The Art of Healing Trauma

COLORING BOOK

Revised Edition

Therapeutic Coloring Pages and Exercises
for Stress, Anxiety, and PTSD

Heidi Hanson

ISBN-13: 978-1985343306
ISBN-10: 1985343304

REVISED EDITION

First Printing, 2017
Revised Edition Published 2018

www.new-synapse.com

Introduction

Get ready to take a relaxing mini-vacation away from stress by immersing yourself in coloring. The repetitive actions and deep mental concentration of coloring can be calming and grounding for the body, helping to return it to its natural state of flow, equilibrium, and resilience.

Coloring is not the only thing you can do with this book, however; you can also learn 9 somatic therapy activities for self-regulation of your brain and nervous system. These activities constitute a basic introduction to "self-therapy," therapeutic activities done at home as an adjunct to therapy. The activities are based on the work of leading trauma experts as well the author's personal experiences managing PTSD symptoms.

Doing these simple activities for even brief amounts of time, such as coloring during a work break or spending as little as 20 seconds doing one of the activities in this book, will gradually build your capacity to self-regulate. This can, in turn, increase your resilience, your ability to easily flow from states of high stress or depressed mood back to an alive, relaxed, balanced state.

If you have PTSD, these activities, and others like them, can help you to begin to have a first-hand experience of reducing the intensity of symptoms that can feel utterly out-of-control. While practicing these exercises, you may little by little begin to feel more actively engaged with, and in control of, your own recovery.

This book also includes illustrations that focus on some of the deeper aspects of recovery from PTSD and developmental trauma (complex PTSD).

While there is an emphasis on trauma recovery, this book can also be used for other anxiety disorders as well as for managing the stresses of daily life.

Best Practices for Do at Home Self-Therapy Exercises

Working with a Therapist
You will get the best results if you do self-therapy exercises while you are being treated by a trained and licensed therapist, counselor, psychiatrist, or other mental health specialist. Discuss your home therapy exercise ideas with your therapist before beginning so you can incorporate them into your overall treatment plan. If you are easily triggered, consider beginning after 12 months of therapy has been completed. Doing any self-therapy activity with a therapist managing your process can make the results more powerful because you will be activating the social engagement system and receiving their support and expertise, deepening the experience and optimizing the results.

Potential Challenges
There are a couple of inherent challenges when it comes to self-therapy exercises:

1. Doing an exercise may increase symptoms such as nervousness, dizziness, irritation, grief or aches and pains. When you place mindful attention on something, like a sensation in your body, it may feel as if it is increasing. Deepening mindful attention may also connect you with memories related to that part of your body. These things are normal, but if you experience them, you might feel distress or other challenging emotions. If you feel you have opened up part of your psychology that is beyond your ability to manage, it's advisable to stop and seek help from your therapist or a trusted friend. Go slowly and carefully monitor your responses.

2. For a self-therapy exercise to work well, part of your mind needs to step aside and manage the rest of your mind's symptoms. If you feel you aren't quite ready because your mind is still too chaotic and disorganized due to the trauma you experienced, please bring the exercise to a therapist and do it within the supportive context of a session.

Journal
Keeping a journal of your experiences can give you a place to express yourself, reflect on what you experienced, and gain insights about changes you go through over time.

Grounding Activities

The Goal. The goal of doing grounding activities is to learn different techniques for the self-regulation of your own nervous system.

How it Works. When grounding, you harness the skills of your mind—focus and attention—as well as an attribute of your biology—sensation—to transform the state of your nervous system.

Calming and Enlivening Effects. When grounding, you will learn, over time, how to use your own willpower and intention to slowly return yourself to "calm alert." Calm alert is the natural state of alert relaxation to which all animals return after being in a high zone (amped up to run or fight) or in a low zone (in a stupor, frozen in fear or numbness).

Reduces Numbness. Grounding helps you emerge from numbness by activating one or more of your five senses—senses that may have gone numb as a result of traumatic experiences.

Reduces Dissociation. Grounding helps you to deepen the experience of being in a body and having a body, reducing dissociation from the body.

Seek Support if Needed. If you find that any part of a grounding activity is triggering for you, please cease the activity and try to do a different grounding activity if you feel comfortable doing so. Also, talking with a therapist about what was triggering you during the experience can allow you to approach the issue in a safe, supportive setting.

1. Drink Something Cold Mindfully

Instructions

1. **Get something cold to drink.**

2. **Focus on your body.**
   - Pause for a moment and take a breath.
   - Focus inwards.
   - Take a sip and pay attention to the sensations of the cold liquid in your mouth. What does the water feel like in your mouth? Does it make your mouth feel cold anywhere?
   - Swallow and see if you can sense anything internally as the liquid goes down your throat and into your stomach. Can you feel any new or different sensations inside? If you don't feel any coldness, that's OK; simply notice that you couldn't sense cold and notice what you did feel. The noticing is the important part.
   - Take another sip and again pay attention. What do you sense on your lips? Tongue? Cheeks?
   - Some qualities you might notice: sloshy, smooth, warm, cold, refreshing, flowing.

Note: Refer to *Appendix A Sensation Words and Qualities of the Felt Sense* for a list of words you can use to describe your sensations and feelings.

Note: If your beverage is room temperature, it won't have an impact that is as dramatic as something really cold would have, but you can still use it in this exercise. Just drink very slowly and sense the liquid in your mouth as you drink.

Other Grounding Activities That Use the Sensation of Cold:
1. **Bowl of Ice.** Get a bowl of ice cubes. Play around with the ice cubes. What are the sensations in your hands? Experiment with putting just your fingers in the ice versus putting your whole hands in.
2. **Bowl of Cold Water.** Place your hands in a bowl of cold water and pay attention to the sensations in your hands.
3. **Cold Washcloth on Face.** Place a cold, wet washcloth on your face and focus on the sensations in your face.
4. **Cold Washcloths on Arms.** Take a couple of cold, wet washcloths and put them on your arms. Focus your mindful attention on the sensations.

This exercise is adapted from the Trauma Resource Institute, "Help Now! Presentation." (lecture, Community Resiliency Model Training, Asheville, NC, July 10, 2016). Adapted with permission.

2. Mindful Walking

Instructions

1. Begin walking.
- **Friend.** Find someone willing to walk with you and walk together.
- **Solo.** If no support person is available, you may do this exercise while walking alone.

2. Focus on your body.
- **Body.** Place your attention on the sensations in your body.
- **Feet.** Notice the feeling of your feet touching the floor or ground. What do the soles of your feet feel like? Can you feel the pressure on the soles of your feet when you step? Can you sense how the pressure goes first on your heel and then moves to the front of your foot? What about the tops of your feet? How is the sensation at the tops different than the sensation at the bottoms?
- **The Ground.** Can you feel the texture of the floor or ground under your feet? Is the ground rough or smooth?
- **Arms.** Pay attention to your arms. Do you feel your arms swaying or dangling or staying in place?
- **Legs.** Notice the feeling of your legs moving. How do your leg muscles feel? Can you feel your weight shifting from one side to the other?
- **Temperature.** Do any parts of you feel cool? Do you feel warm anywhere inside?
- **Air.** Do you feel any air currents moving around you?
- **Friction.** Are any parts of your body rubbing against any other parts?
- **Some sensations you might have:** heaviness, pressure, swaying, breeze, air, or tingling.

3. Talk about what you notice.
Reinforce your experience by telling the person you're walking with what sensations you noticed. Writing what you notice down in your journal can also bring your feelings more strongly into your awareness, enhancing the exercise.

This exercise is adapted from the Trauma Resource Institute, "Help Now! Presentation."

3. Look for Colors

Deer munching on grass in a field have a natural, innate mechanism called "orienting" that helps ensure their survival in the wild. They frequently scan their surroundings, orienting themselves to any signs of possible danger. This is also the case for us. Even though we aren't in the fields or forests, scanning the environment to gather information about safety and danger is hard-wired into our bodies as a mechanism to help us survive. Our survival brain is always listening for information we glean by orienting to figure out if we are safe. This exercise harnesses this built-in aspect of our biology to tell the survival brain and entire nervous system that we are, for this moment, safe.

Instructions
1. Look around your environment and name 6-20 colors you see.
2. It's OK to name the same color more than once if you see it in multiple places.
3. You may name as many colors as you like. Keep naming colors until you feel like you have come to a calm alert state.

Tips for Orienting
*   When you orient, look around your environment slowly, attentively, and carefully. Scan the environment with new eyes, examining things you may never have noticed before.
*   Look in all directions. Look all the way to the left and all the way to the right. If there are things behind you, turn and look at them too. Make sure to look all around so you have a full awareness of your environment—near and far, up and down, left and right, in front and behind.
*   Relax and allow your senses to expand beyond your zone of hyper focus—the tight focus on what is most stressful to you.
*   Orienting focuses your attention on physical things around you in the here and now. Looking specifically at colors of objects makes you focus on a mundane aspect of things that usually isn't associated with anything scary. Allow the stress habit (and potentially elevated stress hormones) to reduce in intensity as you focus on simplicity for a little while.
*   Orienting helps your survival brain understand that there is no danger in your world at this exact moment. This helps you slowly learn to feel inside yourself and inside your body that you are safe.

Other Points of Focus that Can Be Used for Orienting:
1. **Shapes.** Name different shapes you see around you.
2. **Shadows.** Point out shadows in the space around you.
3. **Material.** Find everything made out of glass, wood, or plastic.
4. **Animals.** Find everything related to animals in some way.
5. **Your Own.** Make up your own orienting activity.

This exercise is adapted from the Trauma Resource Institute, "Help Now! Presentation."

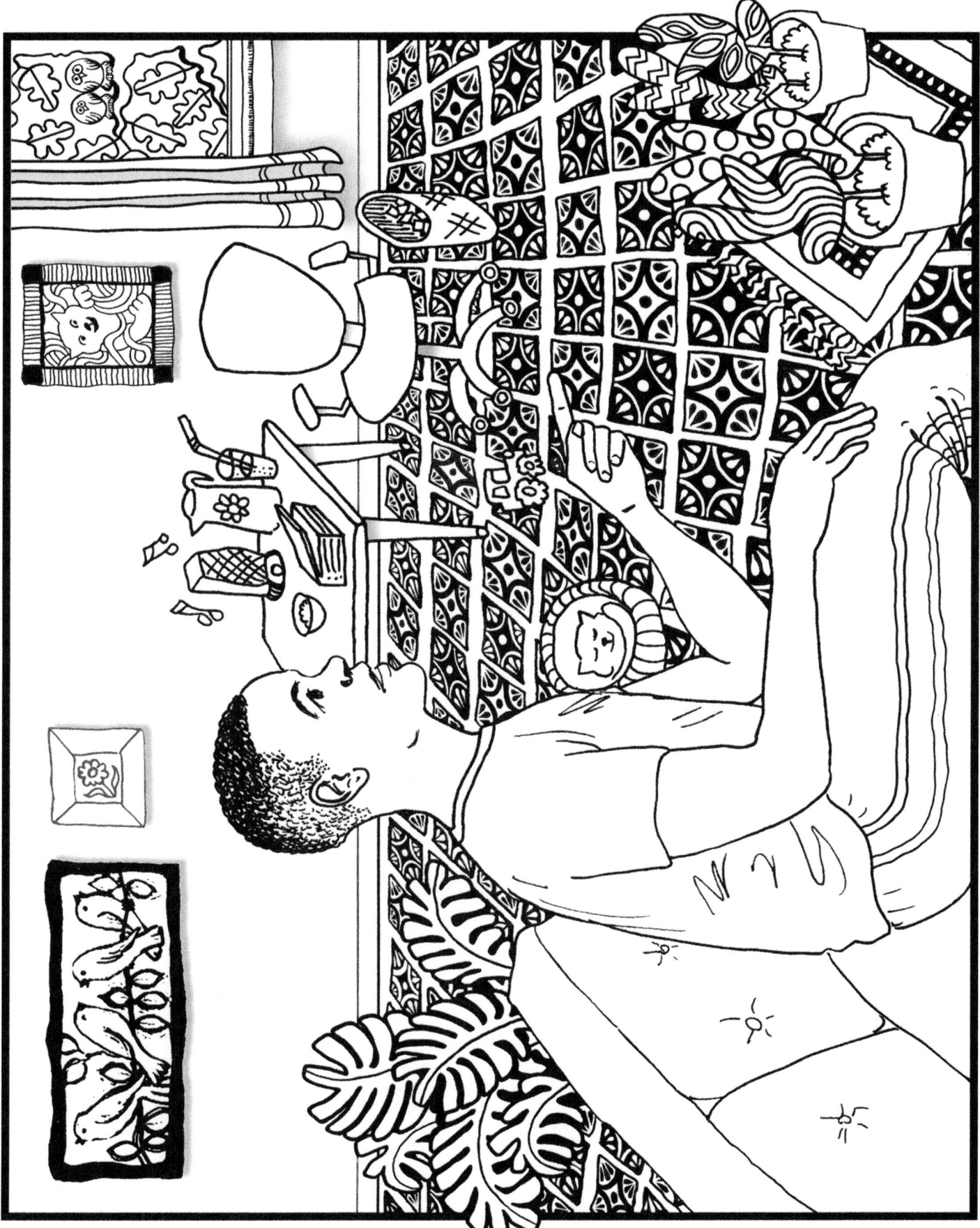

4. Push Against a Wall

Instructions

1. Push against a wall with your hands.
- Stand facing a wall or a securely closed door (one that won't open if pushed on).
- Put both palms against the wall at the level of your shoulders, or whatever feels most comfortable for you, and lean your body towards the wall.
- Push against the wall.

2. Focus on your body.
- Notice the muscles in your upper arms, forearms, and hands. Pay attention to how they feel while pushing the wall.
- Push harder. Pay attention to how your shoulders and back feel.
- Press your feet into the ground. Pay attention to how your legs and feet feel.
- You may feel things like: pressure, strain, tension, contraction, or heat.
- Breathe.
- Notice any sensations anywhere in your body. Pay attention to changes; see what arises in you, what changes its characteristics, and what goes away.
- Let all the stress in your body go into the action of pushing against the wall.

Muscles. A lot of fight and flight energy gets stuck in the muscles, so it can be interesting to focus on what feelings arise from the muscles. However, you can focus on any sensation in your entire body as well. The idea is to be present with your body as it experiences the exertion of the act of pushing and to just "be with" it.

Hands and Feet. Good areas to focus on are where your feet push into the floor and where your hands push into the wall because these points also help ground you by connecting you to the physical world around you.

Fight Response. Pushing things away from you is an action that is part of the "fight" response. If you feel emotions arising inside from past situations in which your body wanted to fight or push someone away, just be present with yourself. If things get intense, please stop to breathe and calm your mind and body. Also consider discussing your experience with a therapist.

Back Against a Wall

Here is another exercise that uses the wall: Stand around eight inches in front of a wall. Gently lean your upper back and head against it. Gradually lean into it. Relax. Sense how the wall and building are supporting your body. Press a little bit into the wall. Allow yourself to notice what is around you and know nothing is dangerous. Having a wall behind you means you can orient to the whole space and nobody can startle you from behind; this can calm the animal mind.

This exercise is adapted from the Trauma Resource Institute, "Help Now! Presentation."

5. Count Backwards While Walking

Instructions

1. Count backwards out loud from 10 or 20 while walking around.

   Children who know their numbers and can easily count down from 10 should begin at 10. Adults should begin at 20. If you would like to have a longer counting session, choose to begin with any number you wish over 20.

2. It is helpful to engage your body by walking around while counting because walking in itself is grounding, but you can try counting out loud while sitting or standing and see if it has a balancing effect on you.

3. When you're done, if you still have not settled back into calm alert, just begin counting backwards again. Keep counting backwards from whatever beginning number you feel like until you feel resilient again.

According to the Trauma Resource Institute, it usually takes 20 seconds of tuning into something that feels neutral or positive to "reset," or settle, your nervous system. In this case, counting is a pretty neutral activity, so counting from 10 twice or from 20 once, covering 20 seconds, could be sufficient to return you to a place of calm alert.

This exercise is adapted from the Trauma Resource Institute, "Help Now! Presentation."

6. Feet, Seat & Back

Instructions

Sit in a location where you will be able to relax and focus.

1. Feet

- Focus your attention on the sensations in your feet resting on the floor. Be curious. Breathe. Begin to hone in on specific sensations. What do you notice? Is there pressure on any part of your foot? Are there different temperatures? Do you feel any sensations like slight tingling, your shoes touching your feet, or air moving around?
- Describe in your mind or out loud the characteristics of the sensations on the bottoms, insides, and on the surface of your feet. (See Appendix A, Sensation Words and Qualities of the Felt Sense, for some word ideas for various sensations.)
- Feel what it feels like to be supported by the floor. Does the floor feel solid? Is there a rug under your feet? Are your feet bare, or do you have shoes on? If you begin to sense a feeling of support, you may note to yourself, "The floor supports my body." You can slide or push your feet against the floor to make that sensation stronger if you like. Feel the floor just a little bit longer than you feel inclined to.

2. Seat

- Focus your attention on the sensations in your bottom and thighs against the surface of the object you are sitting on. Be curious. Breathe. Begin to hone in on specific sensations. What do you notice?
- Let your awareness include the seat of the chair. Now let your awareness expand to include the legs of the chair and the floor. Can you sense that below you there is a place where the feet of the chair are supported by the floor? It's fine if you feel a vague or general awareness. Just rest with whatever sense you have at this moment of the chair and of the floor under the chair.

3. Back

- Focus on the sensations in your back as you lean against the back of the chair. Be curious. Breathe. Begin to hone in on specific sensations. What do you notice?
- Sense the back of the chair. Sense how the back connects into the chair seat and legs and how the legs are supported by the floor.
- These are the characteristics of the specific location where you are located in this present moment. You are in one location and one time. You may think to yourself, "I am located here. I am supported by the floor. This is the place I am located in this moment."

Finish by sensing if there are any ways you feel different now than when you started the exercise.

Remember to Ground Frequently

7. Four Count Breathing

(Lt. Col. Dave Grossman's Tactical Breathing)

Instructions

1. Breathe in while counting to four.
2. Hold your breath while counting to four.
3. Breathe out while counting to four.
4. Hold your breath while counting to four.
5. Do this sequence two more times.

The Freeze/Fight/Fight Response

When you perceive a threat, whether real or a trigger in the environment that is a reminder of a past threat, your system goes into freeze/flight/fight response. Your autonomic nervous system tells your breathing to become shallow and fast in order to respond to the threat.

The Somatic and the Autonomic Nervous System Response

When you step in and use your voluntary muscles to open and close the breathing deliberately and slowly, you are using the somatic nervous system to influence body responses that are generally under the control of the autonomic nervous system. After deliberately breathing slowly for a little while, your autonomic nervous system gets the message and begins to calm down the threat response in your body.[1]

---

1   Dave Grossman, "The Psychological Consequences of Killing: Perpetration-Induced Traumatic Stress." Killology Research Group. https://www.killology.com/on-killing-ii.

8. Body Awareness: Color In Your Felt Sense

Instructions

1. **Create your own color key.**

    - Decide on a color and/or pattern that you would like to use for each of the different sensations listed in the Color Key. Then color the boxes in (color over the words).

1. **Color in your felt sense.**

    - Find a quiet place where you won't be disturbed for a little while and can concentrate.
    - Get into a comfortable position and relax.
    - Focus inward.
    - Notice the sensations you feel in your body right now. Consult Appendix A to remind yourself of sensation words if you wish.
    - Tune into your "felt sense." **The felt sense is the unified, ever-changing, responsive body awareness of all that is occurring inside and around you, from moment to moment.**[2] It is your sensory landscape. When you deepen your experience of your felt sense, you move your focus from actions and things happening outside you in the world to **qualities of your present, internal experience** (e.g. textures, colors, sensations).
    - As you identify the sensations in your body corresponding to those in the Key, color those areas in the body outlines with the color you chose.

---

2   Peter A. Levine, Waking the Tiger: Healing Trauma (North Atlantic Books, 1997).

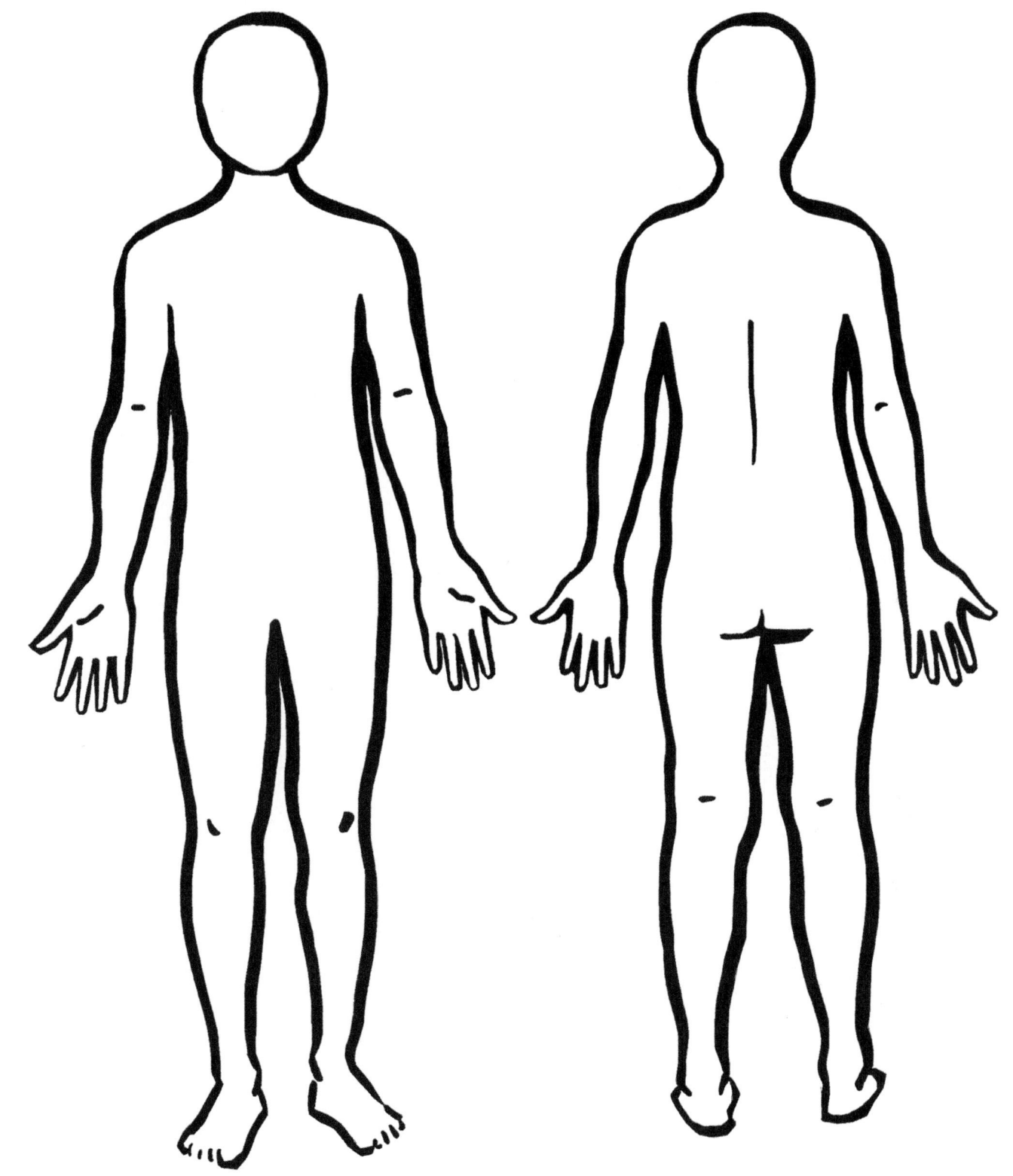

COLOR KEY:

Warm		Tingly		Air Current		Contraction
Cool		Ache	Pain	Heavy	Dense	Expansion
Tension		Pressure		Light		Discomfort
Relaxed	Calm	Diffuse like Steam		Itchy	Tickly	Nothing

The 5 Step Self-Holding Exercise

The 5 Step Self-Holding Exercise is an activity compiled from various sources that can be especially helpful with managing anxiety, stress, and symptoms related to PTSD. The goal of this exercise is to little by little decrease the body's level of activation in order to reach a state of calm alert.

Step 1.
Hands on Sides of Head

As you do this exercise, tune into your felt sense to the best of your ability by feeling and noticing all the sensations as they pass though you—like watching a stream and noticing the colors, shapes, energy, sounds, and motion.

Instructions
1. **Get into a comfortable position.**
   You may have your eyes opened or closed, whatever feels most comfortable for you. You may lie down or be seated.

2. **Place your hands on either side of your head.**

Try Out the Method – Feeling Your Hands as Your Container
Think about how you are creating edges for your thoughts. You are creating the sides of a container that contains your thoughts. You can imagine that you have some kind of actual container where your hands are, like a hat or bowl. This container keeps inside what is important to you to keep inside, and it keeps other thoughts and influences out. You can try this method during any of the other steps in this exercise.

Step 2.
Hands on Head, Front & Back

Instructions

1. **Place one hand on your forehead and one hand on the back of your head.**

   It doesn't matter which hand (left or right) goes in which position. Experiment to find out what feels right for you.

   If you are lying down, you may place 2 or 3 pillows to one side so you can relax your arm onto the pillows as you rest your hand on your forehead.

2. **Feel the sensations in your hands and head. Feel the container around your thinking.**

Step 3.
Hands on Forehead & Heart

Instructions

1. **Place one hand on your forehead and one hand on your heart.**[3]

2. **Focus your attention on the sensations in your hands and body.**

Try Out the Method – Feel the Hands and Then the Body

When you place your attention on a specific area, it deepens your perception of sensations in that area and helps you better sense the relationship it has with other areas.

Hands

- First, pay attention to the hand that is on your forehead. Feel what the hand feels like, inside and on the surface. Is it relaxed? Tense? Warm? Tingling? Feel what the hand feels when it's touching your forehead. Does the hand feel that the forehead feels hard? Warm? What is it like for the hand to feel the forehead? Simply be with the hand; gently rest your focused attention on it for a little while.
- Now feel what the second hand on the heart feels. How does that hand feel? Heavy? Tense or relaxed? Cool on top? Can it feel your chest underneath it? Does it feel that your chest is warm? Solid? Be with that hand for a little bit.

Body

- Feel the forehead. What sensations are inside the forehead? How does the forehead sense the hand sitting on it? Does it feel some weight, warmth, comfort? Sometimes there are no words for what you sense. It's OK. Just be with the sensations as they shift and change for a while, even if you can't describe them.
- Now feel inside the heart/chest area. What sensations are in there? Maybe a little tension or relaxation? You may even sense some emotions, or colors, or shapes, or qualities, like slow wave motion, or jagged textures, or yellow or blue. Maybe a fog or cloud. What does the chest feel with the hand sitting on top of it? Does it feel a little pressure in that area? Some weight? Perhaps some warmth? Just sit with it for a while. Be with the heart for a while.

Was there any difference sensing the part of the body doing the touching—the hands—and the parts of the body receiving the touch—the head and the heart? Did you notice any difference between the two hands? Did you notice any difference between the head and the heart? You can try this method during any of the other steps in this exercise.

---

3   Ruth Buczynski, Webinar: Creating Safety in Practice: How the Right Tools Can Speed Healing and Reduce Symptoms for Even the Most Traumatized Clients. (NICABM National Institute for the Clinical Application of Behavioral Medicine, 2013).

Step 4.
Hands on Heart & Belly

Instructions

1. **Place one hand on your heart and one hand on your belly.**[4]

2. **Focus your attention on the sensations in your hands and body.**

Try Out the Method - Feeling the Between Space

Gently place your attention on the area between your two hands, the area inside your body between your heart and belly. See if this focused attention has a different result than the previous method. You can try this method during any of the other steps in this exercise.

Notice the Shift

Stay in this position until there is a shift.

Peter Levine:

"Then take the upper hand and put it on the belly. And again just wait until there is some shift, until there is some flow, and sometimes people, if they are unable to sleep or they are afraid, they will have nightmares. If they do simple things like that, they will fall into sleep much more easily."[5]

See of you notice a shift occur inside you during any of the steps of this exercise.

---

4   Buczynski, "Creating Safety in Practice"
5   Buczynski, "Creating Safety in Practice"

Step 5.
Hands on Solar Plexus &
Base of Head

Instructions

1. **Place one hand on your solar plexus**—the point above your belly and right below your rib cage—**and the other hand behind the base of your head**—halfway covering the base of your head and halfway onto your neck.

2. **Focus your attention on the sensations in your hands and body.**

Try Out the Method - Intuitive Sensing

Use your intuition and allow your attention to go where it feels most drawn to go. You can try this method during any of the other steps in this exercise.

Trauma Healing
Messages

Wolf Fur

Be very still
like a cat
waiting on a mouse,
like the snow blanketing
at dawn.
Quieting.
Breathing.
Allow the cords of pain writhing
to stop, to yawn, to gaze at shadows dancing on a safe child's ceiling;
allow the panicked what-ifs squeezing your mind
to hold teacups instead
and to contemplate the
steam rising into the air, in a quaint café on the corner of here and here,
now and now,
and draw finger circles on the window.
Still the thoughts
in the midst of their
gripping certainties
their clutching, heart-stopping
march of tears; still them even as the
flags of terror are snapping
in whirlwinds of cacophony.
Be with one muscle.
Be with the bracing intestines;
Be with the heart so lost but beating the rhythm of life
nonetheless.
Be with the tiniest muscle you can find.
Quiet the lies fountaining forth an endless sermon of doubt,
nightmares
upon nightmares
churning stomach
black boxes
of twisted code tumbling from unholy heavens.
Open all the boxes.
Throw their contents into the humming heart of your cultivated presence;
ask the one-who-stands-with you always;
ask the tree whispers falling around you;
ask the small leaves glistening, finding you;
ask the wolf radiating the fierce heat of the center of your heart through its fur;
ask them to hold your entire experience, every moment.

A Message from the Forest Creatures

If you are a survivor of trauma and abuse, take a moment to receive this message from these loving forest creatures.

Inner Child Healing

Instructions

1. **Here you can give your inner child the things below that it may be yearning for. Just color them in!**
    *   play and imagination
    *   to have your deepest concerns validated
    *   love, love, love
    *   protection
    *   listening
    *   wings to fly (meaning support to dream of becoming many things)
    *   appropriate affection (bear hugs)
    *   to be the light in someone's world
    *   consistency
    *   arms to lift you up
    *   safety to feel
    *   a place of honor (There are two big hearts and one little heart. The big ones represent a support network, but not necessarily two parents; they can represent a caregiver, single parent, parent's friends, community, etc.)

2. **Ask your inner child which item in the list it wants to have as a superpower for today!**

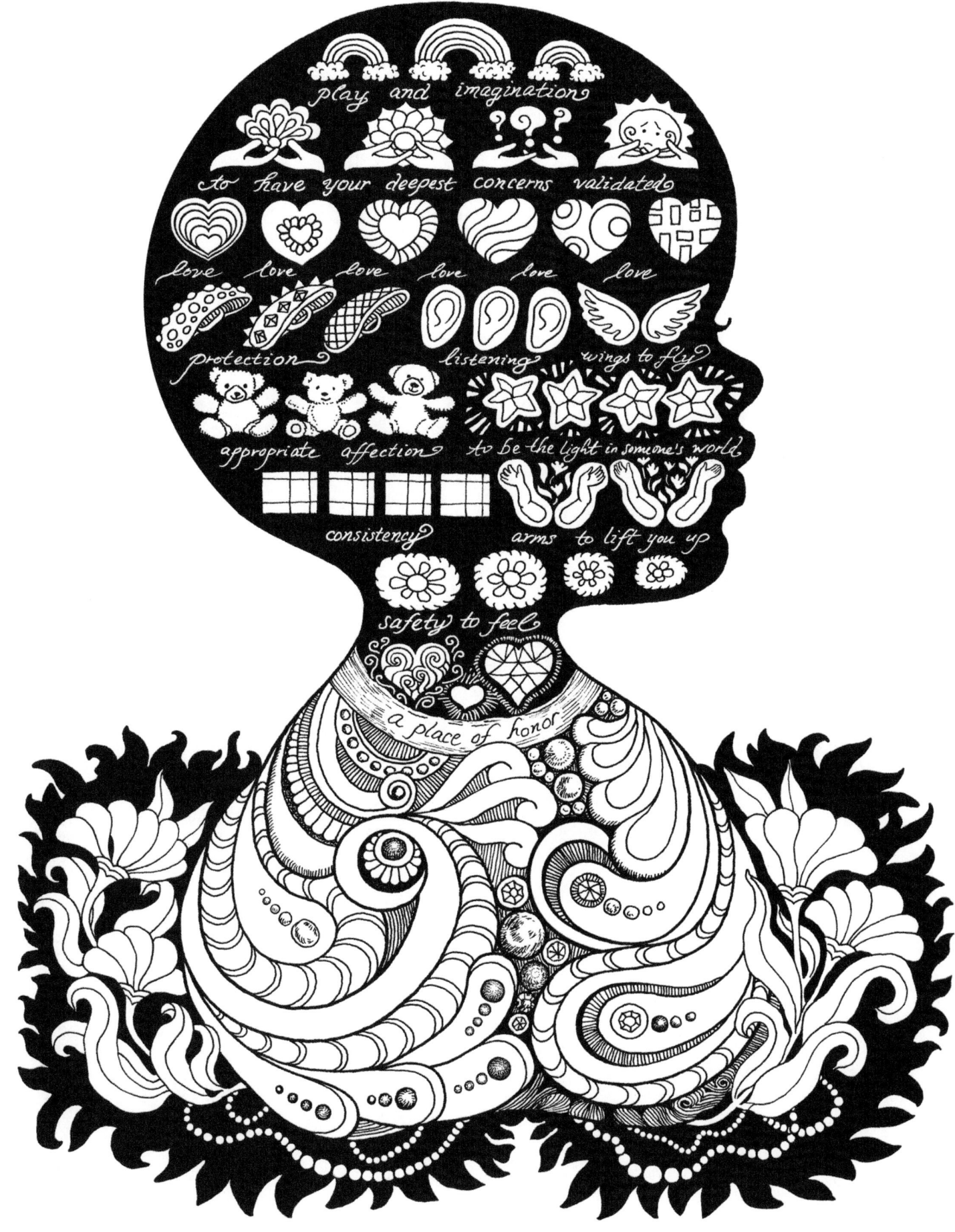

Opening to Goodness & Allowing Emotions

In this illustration, a young woman trauma survivor is surrounded by a wise owl, friendly tree frogs, a happy jack rabbit, some doves, roses, plum blossoms, clouds and stars.

There are two hands, one on either side of the young woman's head. They represent the Inner Nurturer, the part of ourselves that is gentle and kind to us as we heal. The hands also represent people who are Nurturers in our lives, showering us with their love and helping us to find our way out of the thick forest of painful feelings after trauma. In the picture, the tall trees of this thick forest can be seen in the distance as the young woman gradually leaves them behind.

The Nurturers pour water over the young woman's head and face. As the water touches her, it turns into waterfalls, roses and doves. She is learning how to open to receive goodness from life and care from others. There are a few tears on her cheeks; she is just beginning to allow her emotions to surface and flow in this safe space created by the Nurturers and all the other forest creatures.

The owl in the picture symbolizes the wise part of ourselves who understands what we've gone through and the very unique journey each one of us must go on to heal.

The plum blossoms above her represent endurance and gaining maturity, depth, and a greater, nobler spirit through difficult life experiences:

> "In the midst of winter, before snow melts and the swallow returns, plum trees blossom onto the barren landscape, bracing the harshness of winter and reminding people spring will come. Celebrated here is the vitality of life, endurance through hardship, and hope that life will regenerate.

> "The plum blossom has been an important symbol in Chinese culture. As a 'friend of winter,' the plum blossom most vividly represents the value of endurance, as life ultimately overcomes through the vicissitude of time. The fragrance of plum blossoms 'comes from the bitterness and coldness,' as the Chinese saying goes. Souls are tempered in the depth of experience, growing in inner strength and unyielding courage."[6]

---

6   Hong Jiang, "The Plum Blossom: A Symbol of Strength," The Epoch Times, June 12, 2011. www.theepochtimes.com/the-plum-blossom-a-symbol-of-strength_1497107.html.

Finding Your Inner Wolf

*"There's a wolf in me... fangs pointed
for tearing gashes..."*

This is something I told my Mom when I was 8 years old. I drew this picture of my inner wolf, and she jotted down what I told her below the drawing:

Do you remember your inner wolf?

When healing from trauma, eventually we may begin to feel the energy and power of the inner wolf. We may unexpectedly begin to feel rage at all kinds of things, rage bubbling up from deep inside us that has been buried since our trauma. It is really about our having been violated. Our fangs—fangs that are curved and sharp for tearing gashes—might begin to show themselves. Become acquainted with your inner wolf so as to use its fierceness in ways that help you become stronger and more whole. Talking with a therapist about this rising anger is a great step to take. Your inner wolf is fierce and wild. Learn to be its friend, and it will be a powerful healing ally for you.

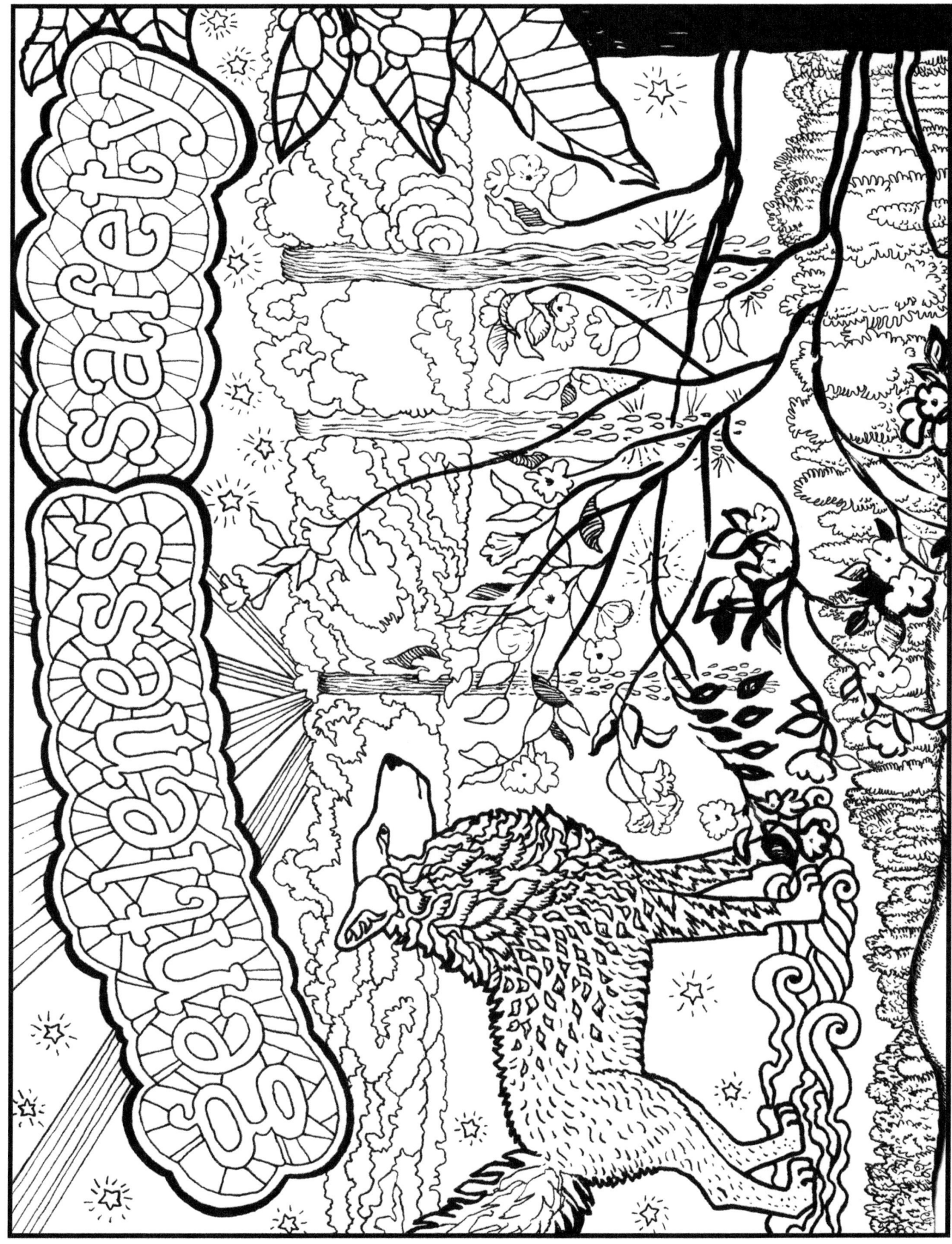

Fireweed

Fireweed is a tall wildflower with fuchsia colored blossoms. Fireweed is one of the first types of vegetation to appear in burnt-over areas, such as in patches of recently burned forest. Fireweed can fill a desolate, charred forest clearing or an entire mountainside with a massive carpet of bright pink.

Fireweed is a crazy plant! It's a plant whose habit is to show up right after total destruction. Fireweed's like, "This is so depressing. So... I'm gonna par-tay!" and then just takes over in its fabulous pink celebration, giving the forest inhabitants a brand new, colorful world. It's also quite a tall plant, pointing upwards like an arrow, as if to point out a higher, wider perspective, one of hope and restoration.

Fireweed

Like fireweed
that springs up in all its glory
after the devastation of the forest fire,
may you
discover a brilliance
still buried in you
that longs to rise,
to feed off the sun,
to grow so tall,
until the ashes become rich food
at your roots.
May you show up
clothed in your bright colors,
full of your soft pride.

Returning to the
Ocean of Life

After traumatic life events, it can feel as if we have been kicked out of the ocean of life and are floundering on the shore, like a fish out of water. We struggle to breathe and don't know where we fit in anymore. The shock of trauma can act like something that severs us from the normal stream of human life and activity, leaving us feeling alone and different from others.

As you color this illustration, think about what it might be like, very slowly and only when you're truly ready, to resume swimming in the ocean of life. Look at the friendly faces and soothing, rippling waves that are there to welcome you.

Appendix A

Sensation Words and Qualities of the Felt Sense:

- **pressure** – even, uneven, supportive feeling, crushed feeling, cutting off circulation

- **air current** – gentle, cool, warm, from right, from left, stimulating, rush, like a feather, like mist

- **tension** – solid, dense, warm, cold, inflamed, protective, constricting, angry, sad

- **pain** – ache, sharp, twinge, slight, stabbing

- **tingling** – pricks, vibration, tickling, numb

- **itch** – mild itch, angry itch, irritating itch, moving itch, subtle itch, small itch, large area of itching

- **temperature** – warm, hot, burning, cool, cold, clammy, chills, icy, frozen, like: hearth, oven, fire, sunshine, baked bread, snow, stone, shade

- **size** – small, large

- **shape** – flat, circle, blob, like a mountain

- **weight** – light, heavy

- **motion** – circular, erratic, straight line, steady

- **speed** – fast, slow, still

- **texture** – rough, wood, stone, sandpaper, smooth, silk, firm, soft

- **element** – fire, air, earth, water, wood

- **color** – gray, blue, orange etc.

- **mood/emotion** – sinking, pulling in, open, closed, uplifting, sunny day, dark cloud, roiling, loving

- **sound** – buzzing, singing

- **taste** – sour, bitter, sweet

- **smell** – pungent, sweet, like rain, like leaves

- **absence/nothingness** – blank, empty

References

Buczynski, Ruth and Peter Levine, Webinar: Creating Safety in Practice: How the Right Tools Can Speed Healing and Reduce Symptoms for Even the Most Traumatized Clients. NICABM National Institute for the Clinical Application of Behavioral Medicine, 2013.

Grossman, Dave. "The Psychological Consequences of Killing: Perpetration-Induced Traumatic Stress." Killology Research Group. Accessed November 20, 2017. https://www.killology.com/on-killing-ii.

Jiang, Hong. "The Plum Blossom: A Symbol of Strength." The Epoch Times. June 12, 2011. www.theepochtimes.com/the-plum-blossom-a-symbol-of-strength_1497107.html.

Levine, Peter A. *Waking the Tiger: Healing Trauma.* North Atlantic Books, 1997.

Trauma Resource Institute. "Help Now! Presentation." Lecture, Community Resiliency Model Training, Asheville, NC, July 10, 2016.
Copyright [2016] by the Trauma Resource Institute. Adapted with permission.

Image Attributions

Printed in Great Britain
by Amazon